First published in Great Britain in 2002 by Brimax,
an imprint of Octopus Publishing Group Ltd.
2-4 Heron Quays, London E14 4JP

A CIP catalogue record for this book is available from the British Library.

Created by *ticktock* Media Ltd.
with illustrations by Chris Hill

ISBN 1 85854 486 6

Printed in China

Presidents
of the
USA

by Ronne Randall

Glossary Words

Look out for words that appear in **bold** in the presidents' biographies. These important words are explained in more detail in the glossary, at the back of your book.

The President

The president is the leader of the United States' government. He is elected every four years, along with his vice president, who takes over if the president cannot finish his **term**.

At presidential elections, Americans vote for the **candidate** they prefer. Then special **electors** from each state translate their votes into **electoral votes**. The candidate with the most electoral votes wins. Elections are a time for great excitement and crowds of supporters meet at rallies across the USA to cheer on their candidate.

Washington D.C.

When the election is over, the president chooses his **Cabinet**— a group of men and women who help him govern the country and make important decisions. The president and his Cabinet carry out the laws made by **Congress**, which meets in the Capitol building.

The White House has 5,000 visitors every day!

The president and his family live in the White House in the nation's capital, Washington, D.C. The president carries out all his most important work in the Oval Office. When it is time to relax, the White House has a tennis court, a jogging track, a bowling alley, and even a cinema!

George Washington

After the defeat of the British army in the **Revolutionary War** (1775-1783) George Washington became the first president of the newly-formed United States of America, in 1789. He was the natural choice as he was a soldier of great reputation, and had led the **colonial forces** against the British.

George Washington, 1789–1797

Born: 1732, Westmoreland County, Virginia
Previous jobs: Surveyor, planter, soldier
Political party: Federalist
Vice president: John Adams
First Lady: Martha Dandridge Custis
Nickname: Father of His Country
Pets: Horses, including Samson, Bluesman and Mopey. Also owned several hounds.
Died: 1799 at Mount Vernon, Virginia

Washington had also been one of the twelve men who wrote the **Constitution**—a document that outlines the political principles on which the new nation was formed and states the rights of its citizens.

By the time he became president, Washington had only one real tooth. He wore dentures made of human and animal teeth, ivory, and even lead!

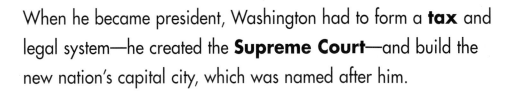

When he became president, Washington had to form a **tax** and legal system—he created the **Supreme Court**—and build the new nation's capital city, which was named after him.

Washington was not a natural public speaker. He was a shy man but was highly respected for his integrity, sense of duty, and strong leadership.

"A knowledge of books is the basis on which all other knowledge rests."
WASHINGTON

John Adams, 1797–1801

Born: 1735, Braintree (now Quincy), Massachusetts
Previous jobs: Lawyer, diplomat
Political party: Federalist
Vice president: Thomas Jefferson
First Lady: Abigail Smith
Nicknames: Father of the Navy, Duke of Braintree
Pet: Cleopatra, his horse
Died: 1826, Braintree (now Quincy), Massachusetts

John Adams

2nd

Adams was the first president to live in the White House. Mrs. Adams hung her laundry in the East Room to dry! Although there was no war during his presidency, Adams knew the importance of a strong navy. He created a naval department and had warships built.

Thomas Jefferson

3rd

"All men are created equal."
JEFFERSON

Jefferson is mostly recognized for having drafted the **Declaration of Independence**. This supported his belief that America should be free from the British, and that all Americans should be considered equal.

Thomas Jefferson, 1801–1809

Born: 1743, Shadwell, Virginia
Previous jobs: Lawyer, farmer, diplomat
Political party: Democratic-Republican
Vice presidents: Aaron Burr, George Clinton
First Lady: Martha Wayles Skelton
Nicknames: Man of the People, Sage of Monticello
Pet: A mockingbird
Died: 1826, at Monticello, Charlottesville, Virginia

Jefferson was also responsible for doubling the size of America when he bought the Louisiana territories from the French, in 1803.

Jefferson designed and built his own house called Monticello. It had a billiards room hidden in the dome, even though billiards was illegal in Virginia!

 **4th**

James Madison

Madison was a clever man who played an important role in shaping the **Constitution**. He campaigned to have the first ten amendments added, known as the **Bill of Rights**. During his presidency, the United States again fought Britain in the **War of 1812**. When the British troops attacked the US capital in 1814, they set fire to the White House. Following a victory for the US in the **Battle of New Orleans**, the war finally ended in 1815.

James Madison, 1809–1817

Born: 1751, Port Conway, Virginia
Previous jobs: Farmer, lawyer
Political party: Democratic-Republican
Vice presidents: George Clinton, Elbridge Gerry
First Lady: Dorothea ("Dolley") Payne Todd
Nickname: Father of the Constitution
Pet: Mrs. Madison's green parrot
Died: 1836, Montpelier, Virginia

 **5th** # James Monroe

Because Monroe's presidency came at a peaceful time for the United States, it was known as the "Era of Good Feelings". In an attempt to keep things peaceful, Monroe wrote the **Monroe Doctrine**, telling the nations of Europe not to interfere in the affairs of North and South America.

Adams, Jefferson, and Monroe all died on Independence Day, the 4th of July.

James Monroe, 1817–1825

Born: 1758, Westmoreland County, Virginia
Previous jobs: Farmer, lawyer, soldier, diplomat
Political party: Democratic-Republican
Vice president: Daniel D. Tompkins
First Lady: Elizabeth ("Eliza") Kortright
Nickname: Era-of-Good-Feeling President
Pet: Daughter Maria's spaniel
Died: 1831, New York City, New York

John Quincy Adams, 1825–1829

Born: 1767,
Braintree (now Quincy), Massachusetts
Previous jobs: Lawyer, diplomat
Political party: Democratic-Republican
Vice president: John C. Calhoun
First Lady: Louisa Catherine Johnson
Nicknames: Old Man Eloquent,
His Excellency
Pets: An alligator and silkworms
Died: 1848, Washington, D.C.

Adams kept his pet alligator in the East Room of the White House!

John Quincy Adams

6th

Adams was the eldest son of second president John Adams. He was a well-travelled and experienced politician but he was not a popular president and achieved very little. However, he did believe in spending **taxes** on improvements to the country, and the Erie Canal and the Baltimore & Ohio Railroad were both completed during his presidency. He went on to become an enthusiastic anti-**slavery** campaigner.

Andrew Jackson

7th

Jackson, hero of the **Battle of New Orleans**, was born in a log cabin in South Carolina—the first president not to be born in Virginia or Massachusetts. Jackson believed he should help the workers and farmers, not powerful businessmen and politicians. He became hugely popular with the ordinary people and won the election easily. He then gave all the important government jobs to his friends, and they became known as his "kitchen cabinet".

Andrew Jackson, 1829 –1837

Born: 1767,
Waxhaw, South Carolina
Previous jobs: Lawyer, soldier
Political party: Democratic
Vice presidents: John C. Calhoun, Martin Van Buren
First Lady: No First Lady. Jackson's wife died in 1828.
Nickname: Old Hickory
Pets: Horses, including Sam Patches, Emily, and Lady Nashville
Died: 1845, Nashville, Tennessee

Jackson was the first president to ride in a railroad train and the first to survive an assassination attempt. He shot the assassin dead!

8th

Martin Van Buren

Van Buren was the first president to be born an American citizen (the others were British citizens), although he was from a Dutch farming family and spoke Dutch at home. Despite his humble background, as president he began dressing in rich clothes and riding in carriages. This made him unpopular. He also lost votes when he opposed making Texas a state, and when he refused to support Canada's fight against England for independence.

Martin Van Buren, 1837–1841

Born: 1782, Kinderhook, New York
Previous jobs: Lawyer, diplomat
Political party: Democratic
Vice president: Richard M. Johnson
First Lady: Hannah Hoes
Nicknames: The Little Magician, The Red Fox of Kinderhook
Pets: Two tiger cubs
Died: 1862, Kinderhook, New York

9th

William Harrison

Harrison served the shortest **term** of any president. On the day of his **inauguration**, March 4, 1841, he stood outside in the bitter cold, without a hat, and gave a speech that lasted almost two hours. He caught pneumonia and died exactly a month later!

Before becoming president, Harrison was famous across the US for fighting battles against Native Americans, over territory.

William Henry Harrison, March–April 1841

Born: 1773, Berkeley, Virginia
Previous jobs: Farmer, soldier, diplomat
Political party: Whig
Vice president: John Tyler
First Lady: Anna Tuthill Symmes
Nickname: Old Tippecanoe
Pets: A goat and a Durham cow
Died: 1841, Washington, D.C.

John Tyler, 1841–1845

Born: 1790, Greenway, Virginia
Previous job: Lawyer
Political party: Whig
Vice president: No vice president!
First Ladies: Letitia Christian (died 1842); Julia Gardiner (married 1844)
Nicknames: Accidental President, His Accidency
Pet: The General, his horse
Died: 1862, Richmond, Virginia

Tyler encouraged many people to move west to settle in the prairies.

James Knox Polk, 1845–1849

Born: 1795, Mecklenburg County, North Carolina
Previous job: Lawyer
Political party: Democratic
Vice president: George M. Dallas
First Lady: Sarah Childress
Nickname: Young Hickory
Pets: None
Died: 1849, Nashville, Tennessee

John Tyler
10th

Tyler was William Harrison's vice president. He was playing marbles when he learned of Harrison's death and that he was now president. A year later, Tyler's wife died. He remarried in 1844, becoming the first president to be married in office. He also had more children than any other president—15 in total! Tyler was not a remarkable president and never shook off the fact that he was an "Accidental President".

James Polk
11th

Polk achieved much during his presidency. He believed in "manifest destiny"—the idea that the United States should expand westward to the Pacific Ocean. A dispute with Mexico over the border of Texas led to the **Mexican War** in 1846. The war ended with a **treaty** in 1848 giving the United States the territories of New Mexico and California, achieving Polk's goal.

Polk and his wife, Sarah, hosted the first official White House Thanksgiving dinner.

12th Zachary Taylor

Taylor was a popular hero of the Mexican War. In a battle at Buena Vista, in 1847, he led his men to victory, even though the Mexican army had four times as many soldiers.

Taylor's warhorse, Whitey, was kept on the White House lawn, where he was popular with visitors.

In 1849, after gold was discovered in California, a "Gold Rush" began. Thousands of people called "forty-niners" travelled westward in the hope of getting rich.

13th Millard Fillmore

As vice president, Fillmore became president when Zachary Taylor died after only a year in office. Fillmore and his wife introduced many new features to the White House, including a library, its first running-water bathtub, and a kitchen stove. However, Fillmore lost support in the north when he signed the **Fugitive Slave Act**, and was not re-elected.

13

Franklin Pierce, 1853–1857

Born: 1804, Hillsborough (now Hilsboro), New Hampshire
Previous jobs: Lawyer, public official
Political party: Democratic
Vice president: William R. King
First Lady: Jane Means Appleton
Nicknames: Young Hickory of the Granite Hills, Handsome Frank
Pets: None
Died: 1869, Concord, New Hampshire

Franklin Pierce
14th

Pierce supported the Kansas-Nebraska Act, which allowed new settlers, rather than the government, to decide whether **slavery** would be allowed in their territories. In Kansas, this led to violence between those who supported slavery and those who opposed it, moving the country closer to **civil war**. Pierce was the first president to decorate an official White House Christmas tree.

Pierce had the first central heating system installed in the White House.

James Buchanan
15th

Buchanan was the only president never to marry. During his time in office, his niece Harriet Lane acted as the White House hostess. While Buchanan was president, the Abolitionist movement—people who opposed slavery—grew stronger in the north, but people in the south were determined to keep their slaves.

James Buchanan, 1857–1861

Born: 1791, Cove Gap, Pennsylvania
Previous job: Lawyer
Political party: Democratic
Vice president: John C. Breckinridge
First Lady: None
Nickname: Old Buck
Pets: None
Died: 1868, Lancaster, Pennsylvania

Abraham Lincoln

16th

Lincoln was opposed to slavery. When he became president in 1861, the southern states broke away from the **Union** and formed the **Confederate States of America**.

This led to the **Civil War**, which lasted four years. Hundreds of thousands of soldiers on both sides were killed.

Abraham Lincoln, 1861–1865

Born: 1809, Hardin (now Larue) County, Kentucky
Previous jobs: Farm hand, boatman, lawyer, postmaster
Political party: Republican
Vice presidents: Hannibal Hamlin, Andrew Johnson
First Lady: Mary Todd
Nicknames: Honest Abe, Illinois Rail-Splitter, Great Emancipator
Pets: Dogs, ponies, goats, a pig, a white rabbit, and a turkey called Jack
Died: 1865, Washington, D.C.

In January 1863, Lincoln issued the **Emancipation Proclamation**, freeing the slaves in the Confederate states. That year on a battlefield in Gettysburg, Pennsylvania, he made a powerful speech asking for "freedom" and "government of the people, by the people" to be restored—he did not want the thousands of soldiers to have died in vain. Two years later, the Confederate General Lee surrendered to the Union, ending the Civil War.

The Union

The Confederate States

However, many southerners remained bitter. One of them, John Wilkes Booth, **assassinated** Lincoln while the president and his wife were at the theater on April 14, 1865.

> **"A house divided against itself cannot stand."**
> LINCOLN

Andrew Johnson, 1865–1869

Born: 1808,
Raleigh, North Carolina
Previous jobs: Tailor, public official
Political party: Democratic
Vice president: No vice president!
First Lady: Eliza McCardle
Nickname: Tennessee Tailor
Pets: Mice
Died: 1875, Carter's Station,
Tennessee

Andrew Johnson

17th

Johnson had been a tailor before going into politics, and was the only president to make his own clothes! After the **Civil War**, his opponents felt that he was too easy on the southern states and did not do enough to help the freed slaves. In 1868, he became the first president to be **impeached**, following a dispute with **Congress** over whether he had the power to make certain decisions. He won the trial and completed his **term** in office.

> In 1867, Johnson bought Alaska from Russia, for $7 million.

Ulysses S. Grant

18th

Grant was commander of the **Union** army during the Civil War. Because he won the war for the Union, he was a popular choice for president. He promised to protect the rights of African-Americans and guarantee their right to vote. Grant was an honest man but had very little political experience and did not choose the best advisers. Dishonest people in his **Cabinet** took **bribes**, which caused problems throughout his presidency.

Ulysses Simpson Grant, 1869–1877

Born: 1822, Point Pleasant, Ohio
Previous jobs: Soldier, farmer, real-estate broker
Political party: Republican
Vice president: Schuyler Colfax, Henry Wilson
First Lady: Julia Dent
Nickname: Hero of Appomattox
Pets: Horses, Shetland ponies, a parrot, and a Newfoundland dog called Faithful
Died: 1885, Mount McGregor, New York

> Grant ate a cucumber soaked in vinegar for breakfast every morning.

Rutherford Hayes

Hayes won the presidency by just one **electoral vote**! To gain more support in the south, he agreed to take away many of the rights Grant had secured for African-Americans, including the right to vote. He did, however, provide schooling for African-American children.

Hayes himself was religious and clean-living. His wife was known as "Lemonade Lucy", because she didn't allow alcohol in the White House.

Rutherford Birchard Hayes, 1877–1881

Born: 1822, Delaware, Ohio
Previous job: Lawyer
Political party: Republican
Vice president: William A. Wheeler
First Lady: Lucy Ware Webb
Nickname: Dark-horse President
Pets: Cows, horses, goats, and dogs
Died: 1893, Fremont, Ohio

> Mrs. Hayes hosted the first ever Easter egg roll on the White House lawn.

James Garfield

Garfield promised to fight for African-American **civil rights** in the south, but he didn't get the chance to act on his promises. Just 100 days after he took office, he was shot by a man who was angry at not getting a government job. Garfield died from his wounds two months later.

James Abram Garfield, March–Sept 1881

Born: 1831, Orange, Ohio
Previous jobs: Canal bargeman, farmer, carpenter, teacher, lawyer
Political party: Republican
Vice president: Chester A. Arthur
First Lady: Lucretia Rudolph
Nicknames: Preacher President, Boatman Jim
Pet: Kit, his horse
Died: 1881, Elberon, New Jersey

Chester Alan Arthur, 1881–1885

Born: 1829, Fairfield, Vermont

Previous jobs: Teacher, lawyer, customs official

Political party: Republican

Vice president: No vice president!

First Lady: Ellen Lewis Herndon

Nicknames: The Gentleman Boss, Elegant Arthur

Pets: None

Died: 1886, New York City, New York

Chester A. Arthur

21st

Vice president Arthur became president when James Garfield died. He was the first president to take the **oath of office** in his own home. Arthur did not believe in giving government jobs to friends, and in 1883 he signed the **Pendleton Act**, which established the Civil Service Commission. People would now have to pass an exam to get a government job.

Electric lights were installed in the White House during Harrison's presidency— but he once got an electric shock, so he was afraid to use them!

Benjamin Harrison

23rd

Harrison was the grandson of ninth president William Harrison. He had been a business lawyer for 26 years before becoming president. This made him a strong supporter of big business—a relationship that is still important in the Republican party today. He signed the **McKinley Tariff Act** of 1890, which protected American businesses against foreign **imports**. Harrison had a stiff, formal manner and was an unpopular president.

Benjamin Harrison 1889–1893

Born: 1833, North Bend, Ohio

Previous jobs: Lawyer, army officer

Political party: Republican

Vice president: Levi P. Morton

First Lady: Caroline Lavinia Scott

Nickname: The Human Iceberg

Pets: Dogs and a billy goat

Died: 1901, Indianapolis, Indiana

Grover Cleveland

22nd & 24th

Grover Cleveland was an honest and hard-working man, who became the only president to serve two separate **terms**. His first term was more successful than the second, during which the country suffered a severe **economic depression**. Cleveland was the first president to be married in the White House, and his 22-year-old wife was the youngest First Lady ever.

William McKinley

25th

McKinley took the United States into the **Spanish-American War** in 1898, to help Cuba win independence from Spain. As a result of the war, the US gained the Philippines, Guam, Puerto Rico, and the Hawaiian Islands. In September 1901, an assassin shot McKinley, and he died eight days later.

> *"War should never be entered upon until every agency of peace has failed."*
> MCKINLEY

Theodore Roosevelt, 1901–1909

Born: 1858, New York City, New York

Previous jobs: Author, lawyer, cattle rancher, public official

Political party: Republican

Vice president: No vice president (1901-1905),
Charles Warren Fairbanks (1905-1909)

First Lady: Edith Kermit Carow (2nd wife)

Nicknames: TR, Teddy, Trust-Buster

Pets: Horses, dogs, snakes, cats, parrots, lizards, guinea pigs, rats, bears, a raccoon, a badger named Josiah, and many more!

Died: 1919, Oyster Bay, New York

Theodore Roosevelt

26th

Roosevelt, a rugged outdoorsman, had led a cavalry regiment called the "Rough Riders" in the **Spanish-American War**. While he was president, the White House buzzed with the activities of his six children and their pets.

Roosevelt believed in protecting the environment and created many national forests and wildlife refuges. When he refused to shoot a captured bear cub on a hunting trip in 1902, toys called "Teddy's bears" started appearing in stores.

In 1906, Roosevelt became the first American to win the **Nobel Peace Prize**, for helping to end a war between Russia and Japan.

The huge rock carving on Mount Rushmore shows Theodore Roosevelt alongside Washington, Jefferson, and Lincoln.

Roosevelt's younger sons, Kermit, Archibald, and Quentin, were nicknamed "The White House Gang" and enjoyed sliding down the stairs on metal trays!

William Taft

Taft loved baseball and insisted on throwing the first ball of the season, starting a tradition that continues today. During his presidency, the Department of Labor was created and a postal savings system was introduced. Weighing more than 300 pounds, Taft was the biggest ever president. A special bathtub, big enough for four normal men, had to be put in the White House for him.

William Howard Taft, 1909–1913

Born: 1857, Cincinnati, Ohio
Previous job: Lawyer
Political party: Republican
Vice president: James S. Sherman
First Lady: Helen Herron
Nickname: Big Bill
Pet: Pauline Wayne, a pet cow
Died: 1930, Washington, D.C.

Woodrow Wilson

Though Wilson tried to prevent it, the United States entered World War I in 1917. The following year, Wilson drew up his "Fourteen Points" peace plan which included creating the **League of Nations**, the forerunner of the **United Nations**.

Two important amendments were added to the **Constitution** during Wilson's presidency: the Eighteenth, in 1919, made it illegal to sell or drink alcohol (this **Prohibition** continued until 1933); and the Nineteenth, in 1920, gave women the right to vote.

Thomas Woodrow Wilson, 1913–1921

Born: 1856, Staunton, Virginia
Previous jobs: Lawyer, professor, college president
Political party: Democratic
Vice president: Thomas R. Marshall
First Ladies: Ellen Louise Axson (died 1914); Edith Bolling Galt (married 1915)
Nicknames: The Professor, Schoolmaster in Politics
Pet: Old Ike, his ram
Died: 1924, Washington, D.C.

Warren Gamaliel Harding, 1921–1923

Born: 1865, near Corsica (now Blooming Grove), Ohio
Previous job: Editor-publisher
Political party: Republican
Vice president: Calvin Coolidge
First Lady: Florence Kling DeWolfe
Nickname: None
Pets: Two dogs, Laddie Boy and Old Boy, and canaries
Died: 1923, San Francisco, California

Warren Harding

29th

With the country recovering from World War I, Americans wanted things to go back to normal, and that is just what Harding promised. But Harding was not a strong leader, and gave too much power to corrupt **Cabinet** members. Therefore, he was not greatly missed when he died in 1923, before finishing his **term**.

> "I know how far removed from greatness I am."
> HARDING

Calvin Coolidge

30th

As a Republican, Coolidge believed that the government should keep **taxes** low and encourage businesses to make lots of money. He was president during the "Roaring Twenties", a time when women had new freedoms and the US became wealthier than ever. These good times became known as "Coolidge prosperity". Despite this, he almost never spoke or smiled and would conduct interviews and meetings without saying a single word!

John Calvin Coolidge, 1923–1929

Born: 1872, Plymouth, Vermont
Previous jobs: Lawyer, public official
Political party: Republican
Vice president: No vice president (1923-1925), Charles G. Dawes (1925-1929)
First Lady: Grace Anna Goodhue
Nickname: Silent Cal
Pets: Dogs, cats, birds, including a mockingbird, a bobcat, and raccoons!
Died: 1933, Northampton, Massachusetts

> At a dinner party, a guest tried to bet Coolidge that she could make him say more than three words before the end of the meal. He simply answered, "You lose"!

31st

Herbert Hoover

To keep fit, Hoover played a game called "Hoover-ball" with members of his Cabinet every morning. A self-made businessman and millionaire, Hoover believed that supporting big business would help keep the country strong. Instead, a **stock market crash** in 1929 plunged the United States—and the world—into a terrible **economic depression**.

32nd

Franklin D. Roosevelt

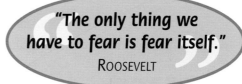

"The only thing we have to fear is fear itself."
ROOSEVELT

Though crippled by polio and confined to a wheelchair, Roosevelt was a vigorous and energetic president. To help end the **Great Depression**, he began a series of programs called the "New Deal". They put people to work on public projects, such as building roads. When the US entered World War II in December 1941, Roosevelt became one of the world leaders who helped take the Allies to victory. He was so popular that he became the first president to serve more than two terms. He died early in his fourth term.

Eleanor Roosevelt was the niece of Theodore Roosevelt, and Franklin Roosevelt's cousin. She took an active role, helping the poor and needy.

Harry S. Truman, 1945–1953

Born: 1884, Lamar, Missouri

Previous jobs: Farmer, store owner, judge

Political party: Democratic

Vice president: No vice president (1945-1949), Alben W. Barkley (1949-1953)

First Lady: Elizabeth ("Bess") Virginia Wallace

Nickname: Give 'em Hell Harry

Pets: Two dogs, Feller and Mike

Died: 1972, Kansas City, Missouri

Harry S. Truman

33rd

Truman, Roosevelt's vice president, was a plain-spoken man who loved to play the piano. When he took over the presidency, he immediately had difficult decisions to make. To end World War II quickly, he ordered atomic bombs to be dropped on Japan. In his second **term**, Truman sent US troops to Asia to help South Korea fight a war against **communist** North Korea.

During Eisenhower's presidency, the Soviet Union launched the first ever satellite, Sputnik I. This started a "space race" between the US and the USSR, with each country determined to be the first to send a man into space!

Dwight D. Eisenhower

34th

An army general and World War II hero, Eisenhower was so popular that he was elected president by the biggest landslide ever. In order to combat the growing power of the communist USSR, Eisenhower increased the number of US nuclear weapons during his presidency. An enthusiastic golfer, he also had a putting green installed at the White House.

Dwight David Eisenhower, 1953–1961

Born: 1890, Denison, Texas

Previous job: Soldier

Political party: Republican

Vice president: Richard M. Nixon

First Lady: Mamie Geneva Doud

Nickname: Ike

Pet: Heidi, his dog

Died: 1969, Washington, D.C.

John F. Kennedy

35th

Kennedy was the youngest and the first Roman Catholic president ever elected. With his popular wife and young children, he brought youth and liveliness to the White House.

> **"Ask not what your country can do for you, ask what you can do for your country."**
> Kennedy

Kennedy's "New Frontier" program aimed to guarantee **civil rights** for African-Americans and improve the poorer areas of America's cities. After the Cuban Missile Crisis, when the US and USSR nearly went to war over Soviet nuclear missiles on Cuba aimed at the US, Kennedy and Soviet premier Nikita Khrushchev signed a **treaty** limiting nuclear weapons.

Kennedy was **assassinated** on November 22, 1963, and the entire nation reacted with shock and grief.

Lyndon B. Johnson

36th

Vice president Johnson took the **oath of office** on the plane carrying Kennedy's body back to Washington. Continuing Kennedy's policies, he began a program called "The Great Society" to improve social conditions. In 1964, he signed the **Civil Rights Act**. But when a military action against communists in North Vietnam expanded into a full-scale war, many people protested and Johnson's popularity fell sharply.

Richard Milhous Nixon, 1969–1974

Born: 1913,
Yorba Linda, California
Previous jobs: Lawyer, public official
Political party: Republican
Vice president: Spiro Agnew, Gerald Ford
First Lady: Thelma ("Pat") Catherine Ryan
Nickname: Tricky Dick
Pets: Dogs, including Checkers, Vicky, and King Timahoe
Died: 1994, New York City, New York

 37th **Richard Nixon**

During his presidency Nixon visited China and the USSR, improving the relationship between the US and these countries. In his second **term** he helped to end the war in Vietnam. However, he was forced to resign in disgrace in 1974 because of the "Watergate scandal". He had been involved in criminal activities and a campaign of "dirty tricks" against the Democratic party.

On July 20, 1969, Apollo 11 landed on the moon. The US had beaten the USSR in the space race.

 **38th** **Gerald Ford**

"Our long national nightmare is over."
FORD

Ford had become vice president after Nixon's first vice president resigned. When Nixon himself resigned, Ford became president without ever having been elected. His decision to pardon Nixon was criticized by many people. His wife Betty, who supported women's rights and was open and honest about her health problems, was a popular First Lady.

Gerald Rudolph Ford, Jr., 1974–1977

Born: 1913, Omaha, Nebraska
Previous job: Lawyer
Political party: Republican
Vice president: Nelson A. Rockefeller
First Lady: Elizabeth ("Betty") Bloomer
Nickname: Jerry
Pets: Liberty the dog and Shan the cat

James Carter

39th

Carter was a peanut farmer and had been active in the Baptist church before deciding to enter politics. His high moral values helped him play the role of peacemaker between Israel and Egypt. He also brought many more women, African-

Americans, and Hispanics into the government. But an oil crisis and economic problems made his presidency difficult.

Carter was a speed reader—he could read up to 2,000 words per minute!

Ronald Reagan

40th

As a former movie and TV star, Reagan always looked calm and relaxed on camera, even when he was nearly **assassinated** in 1981. As president, he reduced **taxes** but increased spending on **defense programs**. Though he called the USSR an "evil empire" at the beginning of his presidency, by the end of his second term relations with the Soviet Union were much warmer. When Reagan said in an interview that he liked jelly beans, sales in the US rocketed!

George Herbert Walker Bush, 1989–1993

Born: 1924, Milton, Massachusetts
Previous jobs: Businessman, ambassador, director of Central Intelligence Agency
Political party: Republican
Vice president: J. Danforth (Dan) Quayle
First Lady: Barbara Pierce
Nickname: Poppy
Pets: Dogs, Millie and Ranger

George Bush

41st

Bush was the first vice president to actually be elected president, since Van Buren. All the others came to power because their president had died or had been forced to leave office!

A year after he took office, Bush sent troops to the Persian Gulf to fight the Iraqis, who had invaded Kuwait. The success of the **Gulf War** gave Bush's popularity a boost. At home, he promised to work for a cleaner environment. However, he could not convince American voters to re-elect him after his first **term**.

William Clinton

42nd

"There is nothing wrong in America that can't be fixed with what is right in America."
CLINTON

Clinton was the first president born after World War II. He wanted to provide good health care for all Americans but **Congress** did not approve his plans. Clinton had more success with foreign policy. He helped guide peace talks in Ireland and the Middle East, and sent a peacekeeping force to Bosnia. But a scandal surrounding his relationship with a White House aide damaged Clinton's reputation.

William Jefferson Clinton, 1993–2001

Born: 1946, Hope, Arkansas
Previous jobs: Law professor, Arkansas attorney-general, governor of Arkansas
Political party: Democratic
Vice president: Albert Gore Jr.
First Lady: Hillary Rodham
Nickname: Bill
Pets: Socks the cat and Buddy the dog

George W. Bush

George W. Bush is the son of the 41st president George Bush —only the second president to follow his father in this way. He is married to Laura and has twin daughters, Jenna and Barbara.

George Walker Bush, 2001–2009

Born: 1946, New Haven, Connecticut
Previous jobs: Businessman, governor of Texas
Political party: Republican
Vice president: Richard (Dick) Cheney
First Lady: Laura Welch
Nicknames: Dubya (W), Little George
Pets: Two dogs, Spot and Barney, India, the cat, and Ofelia the cow

> **"Great tragedy has come to us, and we are meeting it with the best that is in our country: with courage and concern for others. Because this is America. This is who we are."**
> GEORGE W. BUSH
> SEPTEMBER 15, 2001

Bush came to office after the closest run elections ever. After votes in Florida were recounted several times, Bush was finally declared the winner, by only 537 popular votes. On January 20, 2001 he became the 43rd president of the United States.

Less than a year after his **inauguration**, Bush faced a serious challenge when terrorists destroyed the World Trade Center buildings in New York and attacked the **Pentagon** in Washington, D.C. With support from around the world, he sent troops and bombers to Afghanistan, where the terrorist leaders were thought to be based.

assassinate To murder a well-known person because you disagree with him or her.

Battle of New Orleans (1815) One of the only battles in the War of 1812 to be won by the US.

Bill of Rights The part of the Constitution that lists the basic freedoms guaranteed to every American.

bribes Money or gifts given to a person in order to influence their decision making.

Cabinet The people who help the president make decisions. Each member runs his or her own department.

candidate Someone who wants to be elected to an office, like the presidency.

civil rights The rights every citizen is entitled to, such as the right to get an education and to vote.

Civil Rights Act (1964) A law guaranteeing civil rights for Americans of all races and religions.

civil war A war between two parts of the same country. The American Civil War lasted from 1861 to 1865.

colonial forces The army of the thirteen colonies that fought for independence from Britain in the Revolutionary War.

communists Followers of communism, a system in which the government owns all property and there is only one political party.

Confederate States of America A separate country formed in 1861. It was made up of the states that broke away from the Union because they wanted to keep slavery.

Congress The part of the US government that makes laws. Made up of the Senate and the House of Representatives.

Constitution The document that created the government of the US. It was written in 1787 and took effect in 1789.

Declaration of Independence (1776) The document in which the American colonies said that they would no longer be ruled by Britain.

defense programs Projects designed to protect a country in case of war, by using military forces and weapons.

economic depression A time when many companies go out of business, and people lose their jobs and have less money to spend.

electoral vote In a presidential election, the votes cast by the electors rather than by the public.

electors Members of the *Electoral College*, a group of people chosen to represent the public. They officially elect the president.

Emancipation Proclamation An order issued by Abraham Lincoln in 1863 freeing all slaves in the rebellious Confederate states.

Fugitive Slave Act (1850) A law saying that slaves who ran away would be arrested and returned to their owners. Anyone who helped a runaway slave would also be arrested.

Great Depression An economic depression that lasted from 1929 until World War II, and affected most of the world.

Gulf War (1991) A war in which a group of countries led by the US drove the army of Iraq out of Kuwait, a country in the Persian Gulf.

impeached The process by which a president or vice president is brought to trial by Congress. If he is found guilty, he is removed from office.